I WILL WAIT FOR YOU.
YANK

WHOOSH

HELLO...

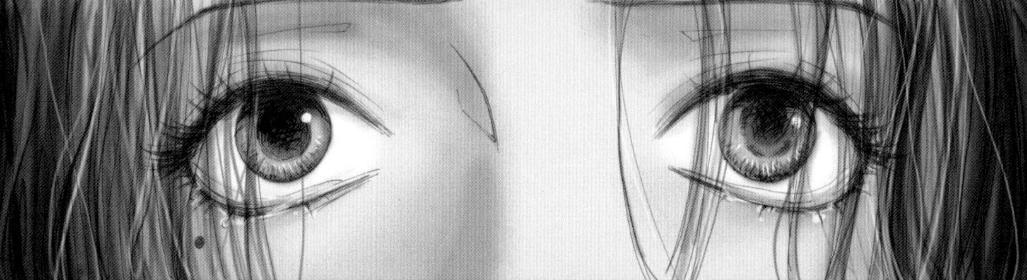

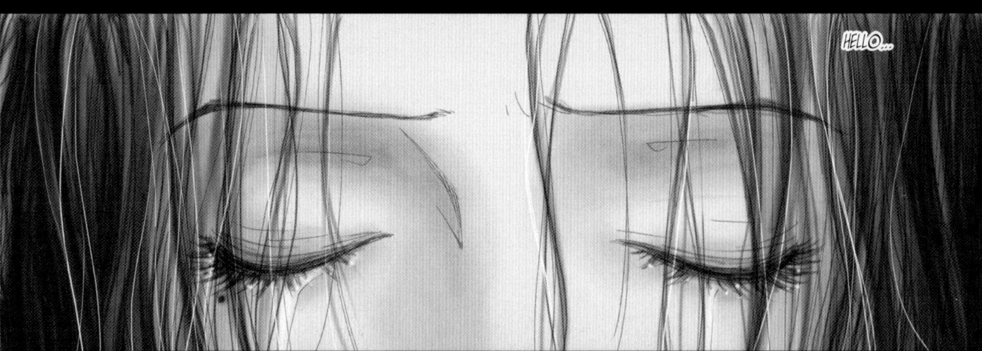
HELLO...

SHE DIDN'T COME.

READING CLUB

VOL. 1

IT'S LIKE BEING TAPPED DIRECTLY INTO SOMEONE'S BRAIN.
Groan
Groan
WHAT'S THIS?
PAINFUL GASPS OF BREATH...
TREPIDATION...
SADNESS...

To those who are faint of heart...
...CLOSE THIS BOOK!!!

GRAB
AIIEEE!!
DROP

PUFF
HUFF
WHY...
...IS HE READING THIS CREEPY BOOK IN SECRET?

HAVE YOU HEARD OF...
...THE LIBRARY OF ALEXANDRIA?
KYUNG-DO'S EYES ONLY SPARKLE LIKE THAT WHEN HE TALKS ABOUT BOOKS.

GOVERNMENT OFFICIALS FROM THE CITY TRAVELED AROUND THE WORLD. IN EVERY CITY THEY WENT...
...THEY GATHERED BOOKS.
ALSO, VISIIORS TO ALEXANDRIA WERE REQUIRED TO SURRENDER THEIR BOOKS TO THE ALEXANDRAN LIBRARY. THERE, THE BOOKS WERE COPIED.
WHOOMP
HOWEVER, THE LIBRARY KEPT THE ORIGINALS AND THE COPIES WERE RETURNED TO THE VISITORS.
Shelve these books please...
BLU-SHING

ALL HE TALKS ABOUT IS BOOKS!
THEY CALL HIM THE SIR-READS-ALOT!
THE LIBRARY WAS SO AMAZING...
Too heavy...
...THAT VISITORS OFTEN FORGOT TO GO HOME! THEY GOT CAUGHT UP IN THE VAST COLLECTION OF BOOKS!
AHHH
FOR CENTURIES IT WAS THE BIGGEST LIBRARY IN THE WORLD. BUT IT HAD BEEN DEMOLISHED BY BOTH THE MUSLIMS AND THE CATHOLIC CHURCH,
OH, NO!

KABLAM
I WISH SOMEONE WOULD DESTROY THIS PLACE!
WELCOME TO MY SCHOOL LIBRARY...
...OR SHOULD I SAY THE GRAVE YARD OF BOOKS!

OH, WHAT'S THAT?
JULES VERNE!
THIS LIBRARY IS RUN POORLY, JUST LIKE EVERY SCHOOL LIBRARY OUT THERE.
AN EMPTY CLASS ROOM WAS PILED FLOOR TO CEILING WITH USED BOOKS, SO THEY MADE IT THE SOLE RESPONSIBILITY OF THE STUDENTS TO PUT THE LIBRARY BACK TOGETHER!
WOW. THIS IS AWESOME!
FFT
FFT

WHEN KYUNG-DO ASKED ME TO WORK IN THE LIBRARY, IT BLEW MY MIND!
YOU WANT TO WORK...
...WITH ME?
YOU!
YEP.
WHAT? WHY?
I'VE ALWAYS SPIED HIM IN THE CORNER OF THE CLASSROOM, FACE BURIED IN A BOOK...
YOU LIKE BOOKS, DON'T YOU?

I'VE SEEN YOU IN THE LIBRARY...
Y-YOU HAVE...?
UGH, PROBABLY READING ONLINE FICTION OR COMICS.
WE'RE THE ONLY ONES WHO ACTUALLY USE THE LIBRARY!
WHAT DO YOU SAY?
COULD THIS BE MY CHANCE? SEDUCTION IN THE LIBRARY!
I DON'T KNOW HOW TO THANK YOU GUYS!

AND SO...
DUN-DUN
...I FINALLY SET FOOT INTO THE GRAVE YARD...
IT'S BEEN YEARS SINCE ANYONE APPLIED TO MANAGE THE LIBRARY! I KNOW YOU'LL DO GREAT!

BANG
OWW!
MY BACK!
Not very seductive...
CRAK
TYPICAL. FACE
BURIED IN A BOOK.

HEY...
THANKS FOR ALL YOUR HELP, THIS LITTLE GIRL APPRECIATES IT...
THIS IS INCREDIBLE.
THEY MAY BE OLD AND WORN, BUT THE REFERENCE BOOKS IN THIS LIBRARY ARE SURPRISINGLY VERY GOOD.
SLIIIIIP
OH...LOOK AT THAT!
IT WAS AT THAT MOMENT...

...I GAVE UP ON THE BOOKS.
CLEARLY, HE HAD NO INTENTION OF REBUILDING THE LIBRARY.
CRASH
SOON, HE STARTED SKIPPING CLASS TO READ THOSE BOOKS.
WE ARE SHORT ONE STUDENT.
DOES ANYONE KNOW WHO'S MISSING TODAY?

I'LL GO GET HIM, SIR!
WELL, THAT'S NOT NECESSA--
NOW, WE'RE SHORT TWO STUDENTS...
SLAM
HEY, KYUNG-DO...?
LIBRARY
CREEAK
CREEAK
SQUEAK
SSSSSSK
SSSS
ARE YOU THERE, KYUNG-DO?

SSSSSSK
SSSSSSK
SSSSSSK
WHAT'S THAT?

SSSSSSK
SSSSK
OHMYGOD!!!!
KYUNG-DO!

HUH?
WHAT? WHY'RE YOU YELLIN--
THUD
WHAT'RE YOU READING?!
Y'KNOW, A BIT OF THIS AND THAT...
......
Complete Masterpieces of the World.
THIS ISN'T THE ONE...

I SAW A GHOST OR SOMETHING.
YOU'RE PROBABLY JUST OVERWORKED, AND THE LIBRARY IS PRETTY DUSTY.
DO YOU WANT TO LIE DOWN FOR A WHILE? HERE, THIS BOOK CAN BE YOUR PILLOW. WHO SAYS ROMAN HISTORY ISN'T USEFUL!
AH, THANKS.
I TOTALLY DON'T FEEL WELL.
A LITTLE REST AND YOU'LL BE GOOD AS NEW.

THE STORY ABOUT THAT LIBRARY. TELL IT TO ME AGAIN.
...
HOW WAS IT DESTROYED?
IT'S A HORRIBLE STORY.
IT'S OKAY. I WANT TO HEAR IT.
THE CRUSADERS WHO INVADED ALEXANDRIA ALSO ATTACKED THE LIBRARY.
NOT ONE STEP FURTHER! THIS LIBRARY IS SACRED GROUND. HOW DARE YOU ENTER!

AND THE OUTCOME...
KILLING...?
THEY ASSUMED EVERYONE INSIDE THE LIBRARY WERE NON-CHRISTIANS. MANY SCHOLARS AND OFFICIALS LOST THEIR LIVES.
THEIR BLOOD SPREAD OVER BOOKS OVER A THOUSAND YEARS OLD.
BUT THE LIBRARY STILL STOOD FIRM.

BUT THEN, THE MUSLIMS, WHO BELIEVED ALLAH TO BE THE ONE TRUE GOD, BANNED ANY LITERATURE SAYING OTHERWISE.
THUS, THEY BURNED...
...THE BOOKS...
...THE LIBRARY...
...AND THE SCHOLARS WHO TRIED TO SAVE IT ALL.
THIS STORY... WAS IN THAT BOOK YOU WERE READING?

BIBLIOTHECA ALEXANDRIA.
HAVE YOU READ THE BOOK?
SLAM
ANYONE THERE?

NOBODY?
WOW. IT'S EVEN MESSIER THAN BEFORE!
SILENCE
SLAM

I JUST LOOKED AT THE COVER.
......
ACK! SORRY!
UMM, WANNA GET OFF ME NOW...?
SHE ALMOST SAW US! WHAT A RUSH!
SO, YEAH, BOOKS ARE VERY USEFUL...

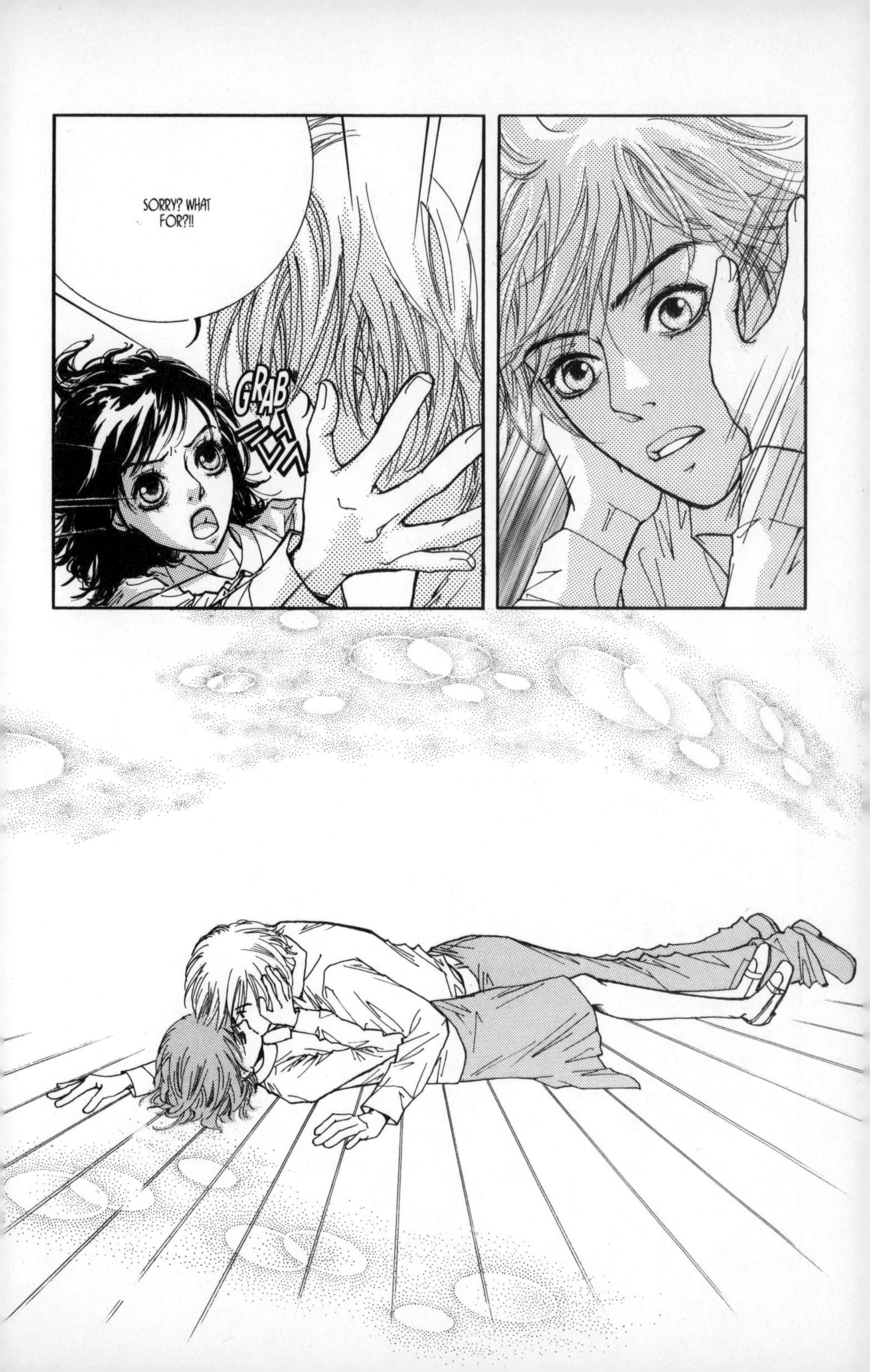
SORRY? WHAT FOR?!!
GRAB

SO THAT BOOK IS DANGEROUS?
MORE DANGEROUS THAN THIS SITUATION?

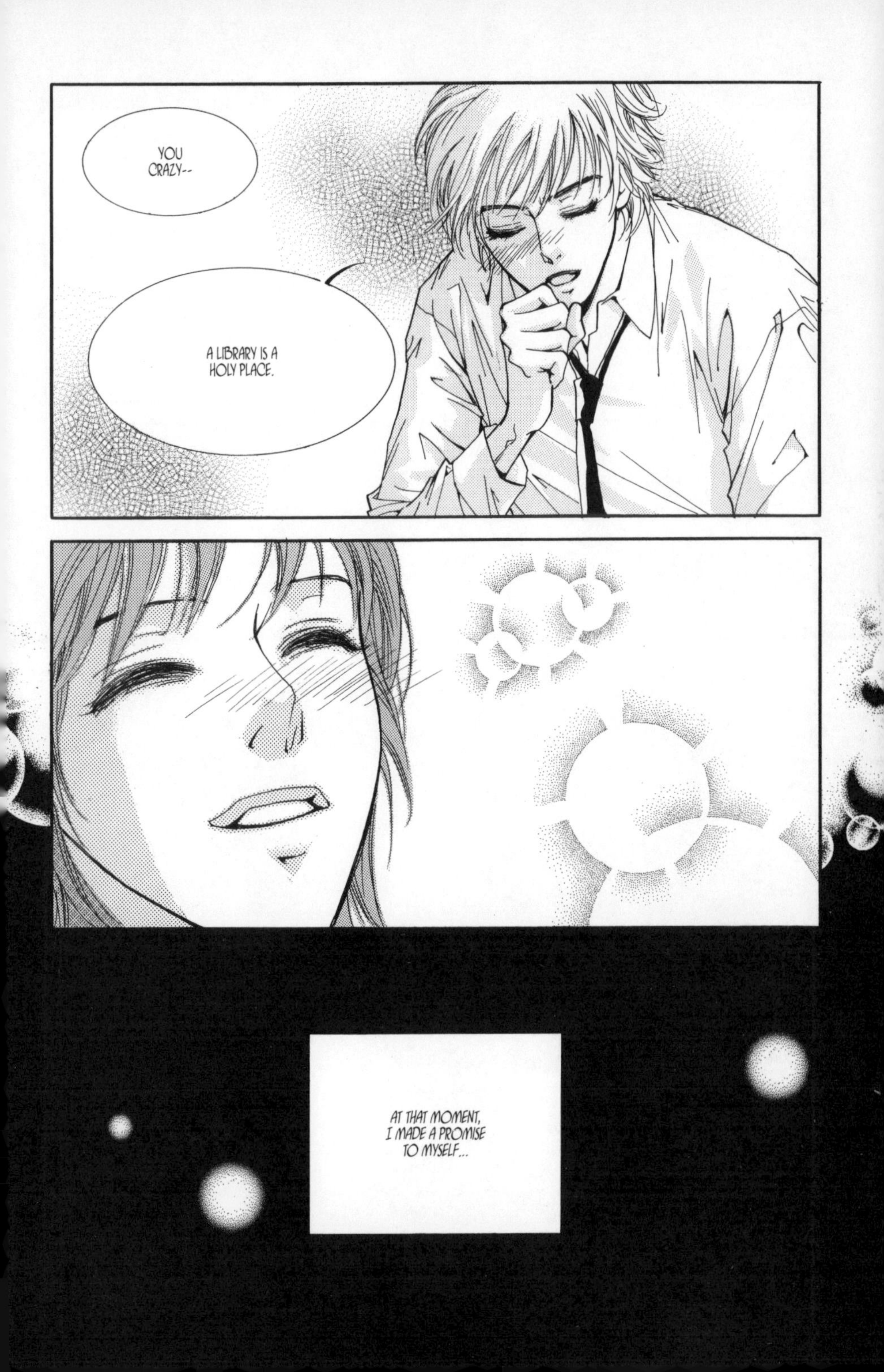
YOU CRAZY--
A LIBRARY IS A HOLY PLACE.
AT THAT MOMENT, I MADE A PROMISE TO MYSELF...

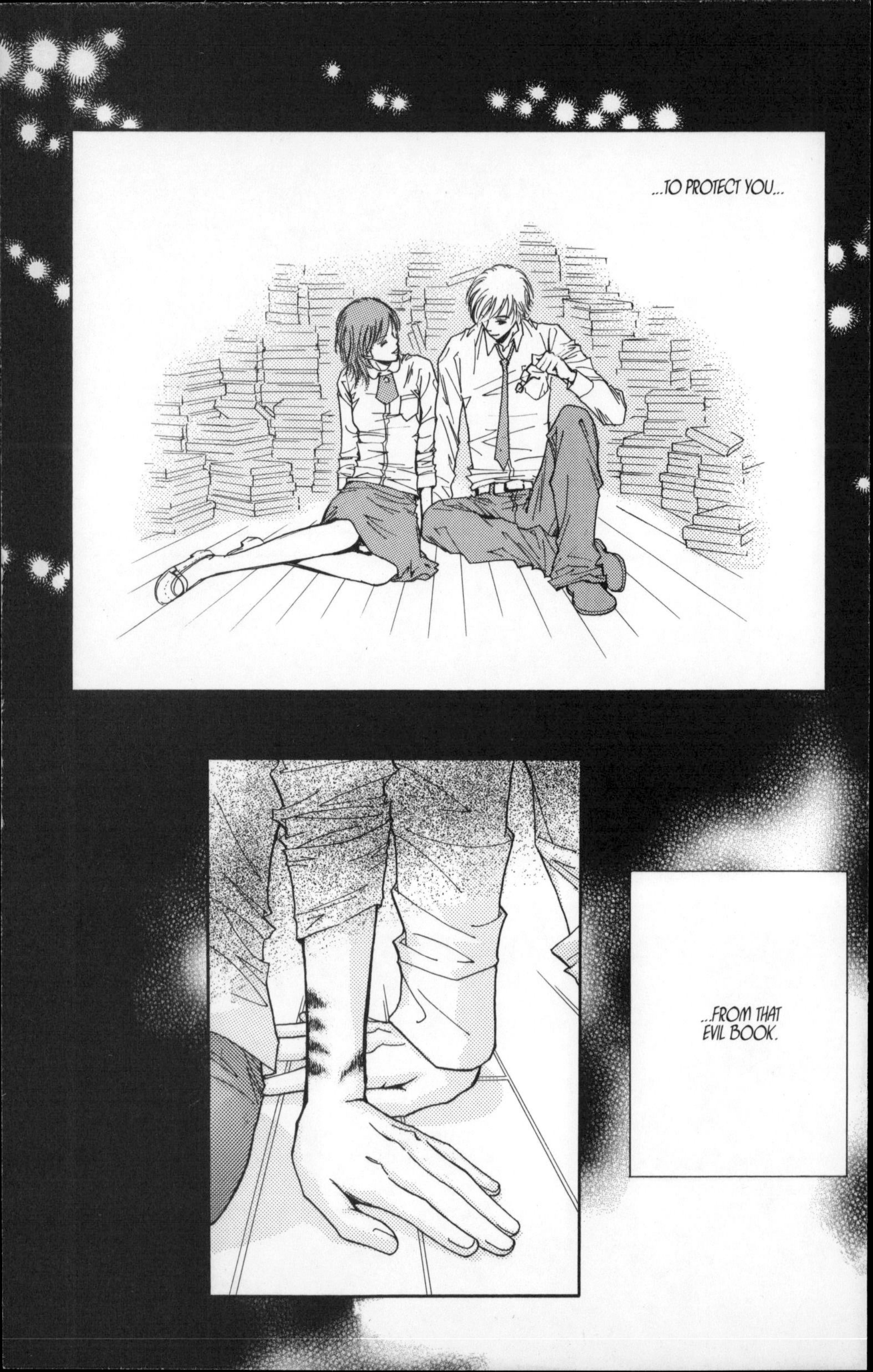
...TO PROTECT YOU...
...FROM THAT EVIL BOOK.

[Illustration: Hieronymus Bosch]

My past is like fallen leaves,
crushed by the memory
of a horrible season.

There is no faltering,
there is no fear. I now open
the first page and take a step
into the dead empire built
with blood.

[Illustration: Hieronymus Bosch]

CRACKLE
CRACKLE
WELCOME TO ALEXANDRIA. YOU KNOW THE RULE OF ALEXANDRIA, DON'T YOU?
A MONK FROM A DISTANT LAND.
THIS BOOK NEEDS SANCTUARY.
A BOOK OF ANCIENT SORCERY?
I'LL COPY THIS BOOK IMMEDIATELY.

HEH- HEH- HEH
DO YOU THINK THAT'S POSSIBLE, HUH?
YES...
I THINK HE'S DELUSIONAL...
I'M SORRY. I HAD PROBLEMS READING THE LAST PAGE OF THE BOOK.
PLEASE, IF YOU CAN GRANT ME A FEW MORE MINUTES TO TRY AND DECIPHER THE WORDS...
HE STARED AT THE LAST PAGE FOR A LONG WHILE.

SPLAT
PITTER-PATER
YOU REALLY ARE A DEVIL!
HEH- HEH- HEH
BWA-HA-HA-HA
YES! IF YOU WANT ME, COME GET ME!!!
H-HA-HA-HA-HA-HA

TOK
TOK
WHAT ARE YOU DOING!
THAT'S DANGEROUS!
GRAB
CRACKLE CRACKLE

ARGHHHH!!!
AND NOW...
...I EMBRACE IMMORTALITY.

DO NOT TOUCH THE BOOK!!
IT MUST BE SEALED AWAY IN THE VAULT OF FORBIDDEN BOOKS. NO ONE MAY LAY A HAND ON IT.
YOU MUST NEVER UTTER A WORD OF WHAT YOU'VE JUST SEEN...

...UNTIL THE DAY YOU DIE. NO, NOT EVEN BEYOND THE GRAVE.
AND THAT'S HOW FAR I'VE READ.
FWOOOOSH

AIEEEEE!
PHEW
HOW MUCH FURTHER HAS KYUNG-DO READ?
WHOOOOSH

WHAT-CHA READING?
TRUMAN CAPOTE.
"IN COLD BLOOD"
WHAT'S IT ABOUT?
A TRUE STORY ABOUT THE MURDER OF AN ENTIRE FAMILY IN 1950'S AMERICA.
IT'S DESCRIBED IN VIVID DETAIL.
EEK! AND IT'S CALLED "IN COLD BLOOD"?

NO, THE COLD BLOODED PERSON IS TRUMAN HIMSELF.
HE USED HIS FAME TO GAIN THE TRUST OF A CONDEMNED CRIMINAL, PROMISING TO SAVE HIM FROM THE DEATH PENALTY. BUT HE USED THE MAN'S EXECUTION FOR THE ENDING OF HIS BOOK.
YET, THE CRIMINAL LIVES ON, WHENEVER THE BOOK IS READ.
IT'S SORT OF LIKE IMMORTALITY.
I GUESS TRUMAN KEPT HIS PROMISE AFTER ALL...
THIS BOY. HIS EYES SPARKLE AGAIN.

AND NOW...
...I EMBRACE IMMORTALITY.
SLAP
OWW! WHAT THE HELL'S THAT FOR?
NO MORE HIDING! I WANT THE TRUTH!!
THE BOOK ABOUT THE LIBRARY OF ALEXANDRIA! WHAT ARE YOU GOING TO DO WITH IT?

YOU HAVE TO DESTROY IT! IT'S EVIL!!
Just burn it, or something!
RIGHT NOW, I DON'T KNOW. BUT I WILL, SOON ENOUGH...
NO, NOT YET.
I SHARE A DEEP BOND WITH THAT BOOK...
...FROM A LONG TIME AGO.

AT ONCE, WE COULD FEEL A BAD SPIRIT COMING UPON US.
CAN I...PROTECT KYUNG-DO?
DRIP

DRIP.
DRIP

WHO...ARE YOU...?

SHHHHH

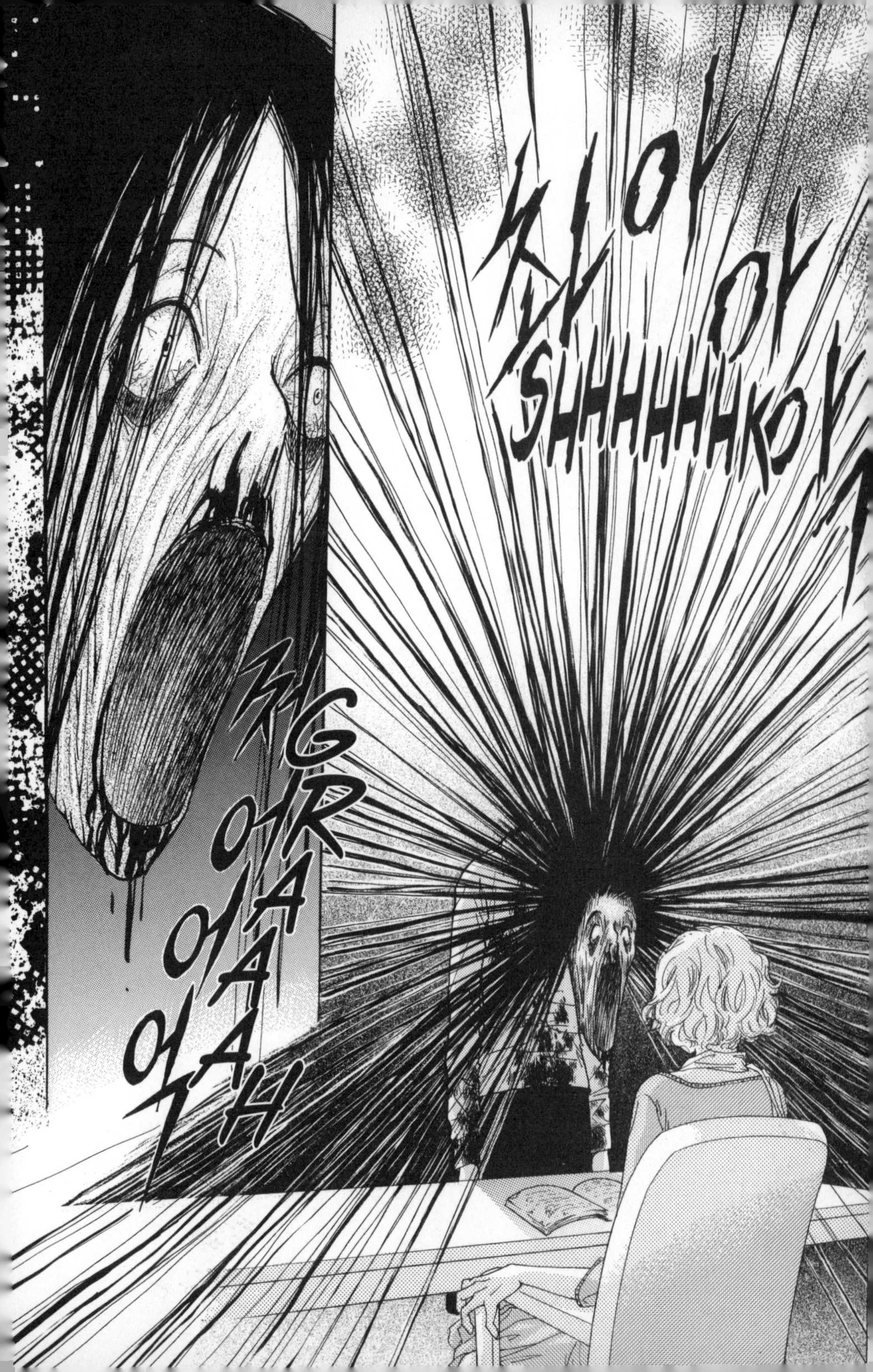
SHHHHHKOY
GRAAAAH

CLANG
IS THAT THE LIBRARY?
HUH? TEACHER?
WHOOOOOSH

WHAT'S SHE DOING?

OH MY GOD!
SHE'S JUMPING !!!
SPLATTO
NOOO!!
CALL 911!!

PANT
PANT
DON'T...
...TAKE ME...

THAT GIRL...
...HAS...NO TONGUE.

[Illustration: Hieronymus Bosch]

My body became dust and
flew away, my spirit
remained as the blade of a
knife engraved my epitaph.

[Illustration: Hieronymus Bosch]

POLICE LINE
FWIP
PHZZZZZ
FLASH

BEEP BEEP

YOU...
YOU'RE SCHOOL ALUMNI, AREN'T YOU?

입금지 · POLICE LINE · 수사중
출입금지 ·

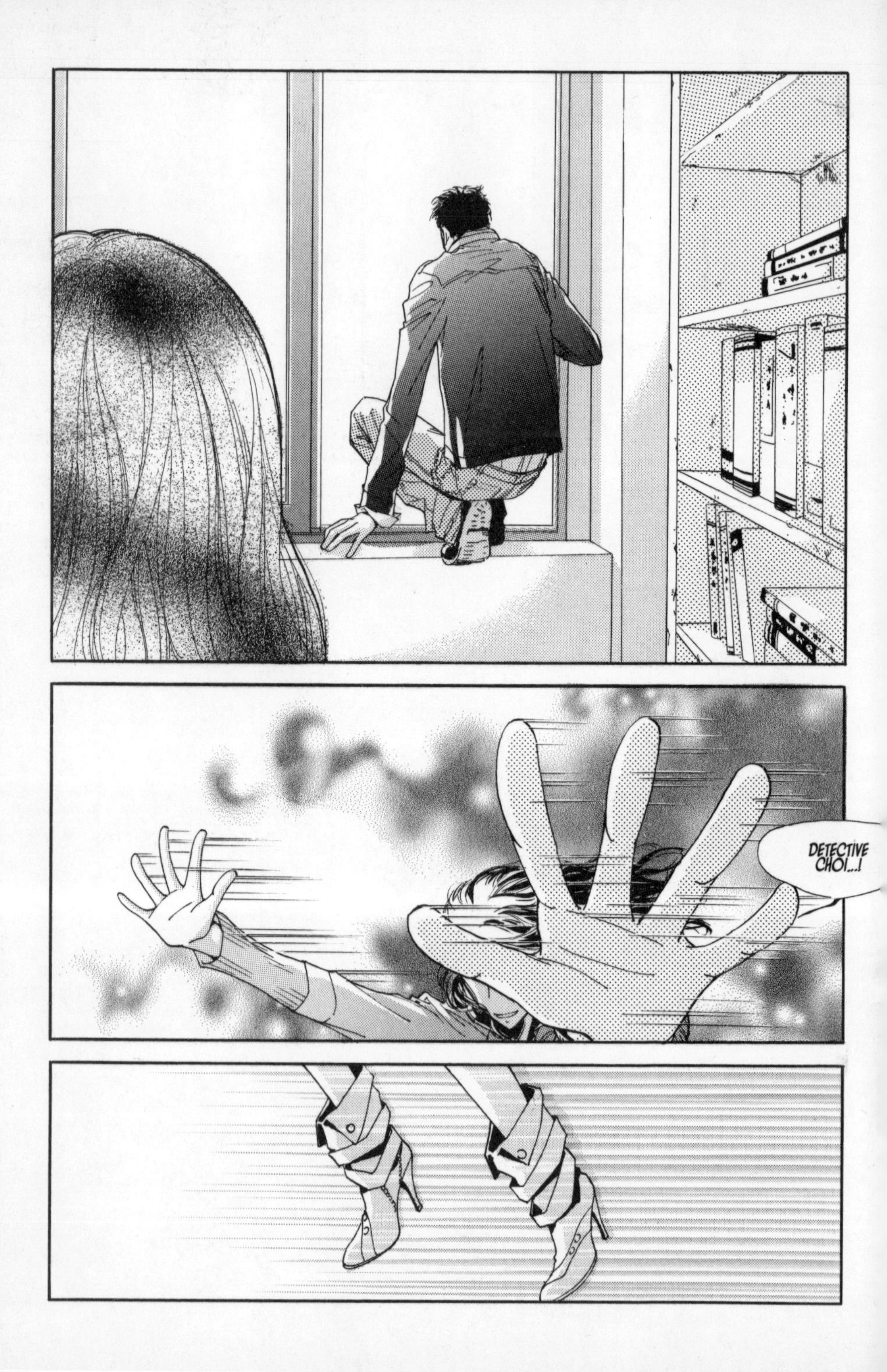
DETECTIVE CHOI...!

WHAT'S UP?
SWISH
AIIEE!
AHHHH!
ARGH
HOLD ME TIGHTER.
ANOTHER JUMPER?

GASP GASP GASP
GASP GASP
SO...SHE DIDN'T COMMIT SUICIDE? WHY DID SHE JUMP, THEN? HAD SHE LOST HER MIND?
I almost died!
SHOULDN'T YOU BE WAITING FOR THE BODY AT THE MORGUE?
TAP TAP
JUST VISITING MY ALMA MATER...
LEAVE. NOW!

SO, ANY IDEAS?
WE CAN RULE OUT A SECOND PERSON PUSHING HER. THERE'S NO EVIDENCE OF THAT.
WITNESSES CLAIM SHE STEPPED OFF OF HER OWN VOLITION.
SO, IT'S SUICIDE. CASE CLOSED.
DETECTIVE CHOI, THESE STUDENTS WORK IN THE LIBRARY.

EUN-SAE? KYUNG-DO?
HAVE YOU TWO WITNESSED ANYTHING STRANGE IN THE LIBRARY?
ANY PREMONITIONS OF A HORRIBLE EVENT?
ZOOM

PLEASE. TELL ME.
YOU KNOW WHY...
...YOUR TEACHER DIED, DON'T YOU?
CLIK-CLAK

HUSH
WELL, CAN I VENTURE A GUESS?
IN THIS LIBRARY...

...THERE LIVES A GHOST.

OOH HHH!
SO CUTE.
GRAB
YIPES!
MY BAD!

WHY DID YOU LET THEM GO?
I WAS ON TO SOMETHING!
WHEN I MENTIONED THE GHOST...
...THEY WERE TOTALLY FLABBERGASTED.
I'm a good actress... yes?
WHAT THE HELL WAS ALL THAT GHOST GARBAGE?
Is this a game to you?

EXCUSE ME?! I'LL HAVE YOU KNOW MY JOKES STEM FROM FINELY HONED DETECTIVE INTUITION!
Okay, it's kinda funny, but...
CAN I BE FRANK WITH YOU?
STOP!!
그만
THERE REALLY IS A GHOST IN THE LIBRARY!
WHEN I WAS A STUDENT, THE RUMOR WAS ALL OVER THE SCHOOL!
SOMEONE REALLY SAW A GHOST IN THE LIBRARY!

THE STORY GOES, THAT A LONE STUDENT REMAINED IN THE LIBRARY LONG AFTER IT WAS CLOSED.
UMM. LIBRARY'S CLOSED.
SHE DIDN'T MOVE A MUSCLE, AND IGNORED THE OTHER STUDENT'S CALLS.
EXCUSE ME, CAN YOU HEAR ME?
HEY, YOU.
SHH-
-HHK

MUFFLE
I SAID STOP IT!
IN FACT, A LONG TIME AGO...

IT WAS IN THAT SEAT, RIGHT THERE...
...ONE STUDENT COMMITTED SUICIDE HERE.
SHE TOO, WAS IN CHARGE OF THE LIBRARY.
SHE DIED ALONE, IN SILENCE...

HOW COULD SHE...?
WAS SHE...YOUR FRIEND?

WHY DID YOU DO IT?
YOU'RE NOT SUPPOSED TO TAKE THAT BOOK FROM THE LIBRARY!
I'M SORRY. BUT I STILL NEED IT.

TELL ME...
...WHAT'S SO IMPORTANT ABOUT THAT BOOK.
HEY, KYUNG-DO!
LOOKS LIKE DAD BROUGHT HOME ANOTHER INTERESTING BOOK!

SO...
LET'S NOT DISTURB YOUR FATHER, OKAY?
IT WAS ON THAT DAY, THAT BOOK CHANGED OUR LIVES.

[Illustration: Hieronymus Bosch]

"Did you say immortality?"

"Yes, I did. Human life is too short. It's lighter than dust lost in the breeze. If you have bravery that can break the sandglass you give yourself, and then if you give me your soul, I will grant you a great power as a reward. The power is never gone forever. It's immortal."

[Illustration: Hieronymus Bosch]

I WAS SO CURIOUS ABOUT THE BOOK.
THUMP THUMP THUMP THUMP THUMP
DAD'S STUDY ROOM?

MOMMY, I THINK DAD HAS SOME VISITORS IN THE STUDY.
WHAT? THAT'S STRANGE.
DAD...?

KYUNG-DO, DON'T DISTURB YOUR FATHER!
FOOTPRINTS...?

KYUNG-DO!!
쿵쿵쿵
THUMP THUMP THUMP
HUFF—

SCARED, FOR NOTHING!
C'MON, BACK DOWNSTAIRS WE GO.

MOM...?
WHAT ARE THOSE THINGS AROUND DAD?

쿵 THUMP
쿵 THUMP
쿵 THUMP
쿵 THUMP
쿵 THUMP
쿵
쿵 THUMP
쿵 THUMP
쿵 THUMP

DRIP
DAD!!!

KYUNG-DO...

THIS BOOK...
...IS YOURS... FOREVER.

KYUNG-D
DON'T LOO

SHHING

KYUNG-DO...
I-IT'S OKAY...
E-EYES CLOSED...
JUST DON'T... OPEN YOUR EYES...
SHAKE SHAKE
SHAKE
MOM... I'M ALRIGHT.
NO, NOT YET.
THUMP
THUMP
THUMP
THUM

THEY ARE WALKING...
THUMP
THUMP
THUMP
...BY MOM AND ME.
THUMP
THUMP
THUMP
THEY ARE ALL LEAVING...
DAD...
DAD...

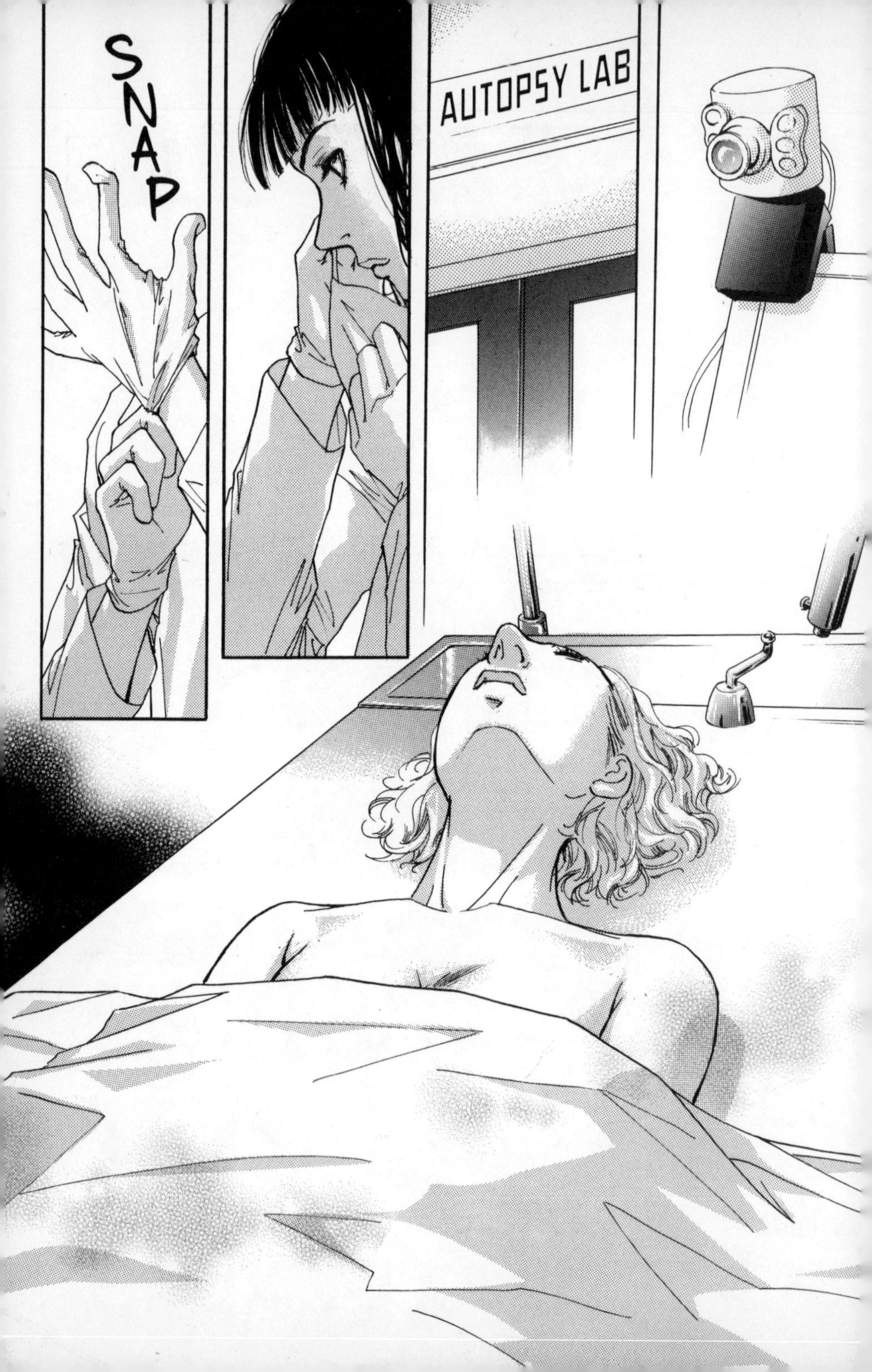
SNAP
AUTOPSY LAB

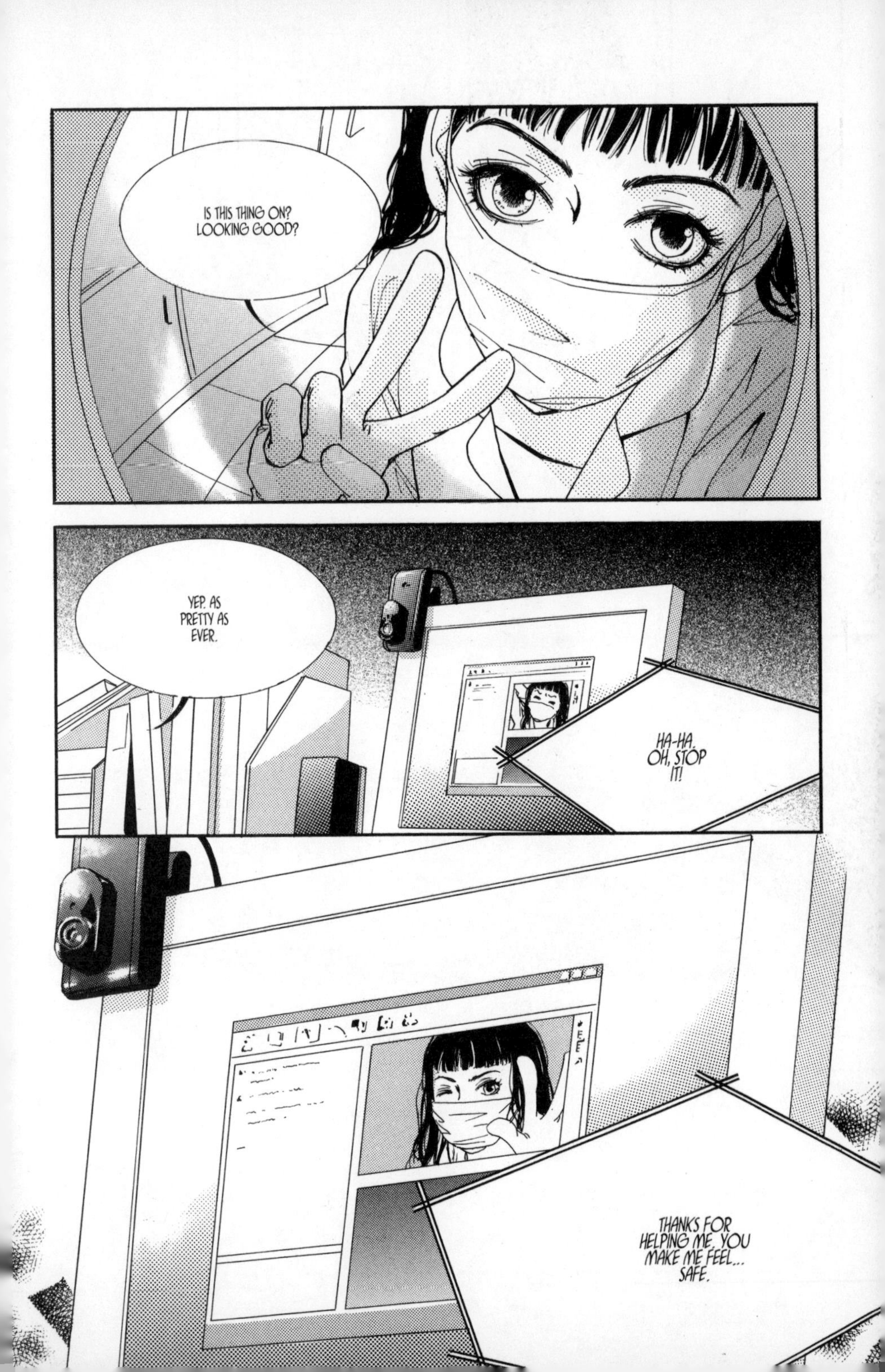
IS THIS THING ON? LOOKING GOOD?
YEP. AS PRETTY AS EVER.
HA-HA. OH, STOP IT!
THANKS FOR HELPING ME. YOU MAKE ME FEEL... SAFE.

I FEEL TOO CLOSE TO THIS CASE.
WOW, SUCH MODESTY FROM THE BIG SHOT CORONER!
I REALLY NEED YOUR OBJECTIVE ADVICE.
I SHOULD BE THANKING YOU FOR THIS JOB!
DID YOU KNOW HER?
...I JUST HAVE A BAD FEELING ABOUT THIS.
NO, NOT REALLY...

SO, WE GOOD TO GO?
OKAY, THEN.
SQUEAK
LET'S DO THIS!

MY SINCEREST APOLOGIES THAT WE COULDN'T ATTEND THE FUNERAL.
AFTER MY FATHER'S FUNERAL, TWO STRANGERS PAID US A VISIT.
WE WERE MEMBERS OF HIS READING CLUB. I'M SORRY IF THIS ISN'T THE MOST PRUDENT TIME...
...HOWEVER, WE CAME HERE TO COLLECT A BOOK HE BORROWED FROM US.

THANK YOU FOR YOUR COOPERATION IN SPITE OF THE TRAGIC CIRCUMSTANCES.
WINK
HI, GOOD LOOKIN'.

FWIP
KYUNG-DO!!
YOU CAN'T HAVE IT!
MY DAD GAVE IT TO ME!!

KYUNG-DO! NO!
DON'T TOUCH THE BOOK!

I CAN'T TAKE THIS ANYMORE! I COULDN'T BEAR LOSING YOU AS WELL!
JUST LET THEM HAVE IT, SON.

YOU DO HAVE A RIGHT TO CLAIM THIS BOOK...
YOU REMIND ME OF YOUR FATHER.
WHY DON'T WE KEEP IT IN A SAFE PLACE FOR YOU?
YOU CAN COME VISIT US WHENEVER YOU WANT TO READ IT.

Reading Club

[Illustration: Hieronymus Bosch]

What do you think of deathless life? My dear friend, I say this place is a river brimming with death, a life of burning fire taking souls, a breathless moment, an unavoidable swamp of agony and an eternal hell.

But if thy desire...

No. Perhaps you've already chosen...

[Illustration: Hieronymus Bosch]

WON'T YOU COME TO THE LIBRARY?
......
NO, NEVER AGAIN.

쾅
THUMP
쾅
THUMP
쾅
THUMP
THUMP
쾅
THUMP
쾅
LIBRARY
쾅
BANG
HUFF-PUFF

HOW FOOLISH YOU ARE.

WHY ARE YOU STILL WAITING FOR ME?
SPLOOCH

DRIP
DRIP

EUN-KYUNG!!
POP

빠각
SNAP

PLOP

TONGUE?
ARGHHHHH!!

YOUR INFATUATION WITH THE DEAD ISN'T NORMAL, HMM?
IT'S IMMORAL, REALLY...
I'M CONVERSING WITH THE DEAD. CORONER BASIC THEORY, 101.
WOW. MY JOB'S GOING TO BE OBSOLETE.
SO...SHOULD I TAKE THIS DEAD BODY'S STATEMENT?

SHE SAYS SHE WANTS TO TALK WITH YOU, FACE TO FACE. COME CLOSER.
THAT'S NOT FUNNY!

FOR SOMEONE CONTEMPLATING SUICIDE, SHE DIDN'T DO ANYTHING OUT OF THE ORDINARY.
NO NARCOTIC SUBSTANCES IN HER DIGESTIVE SYSTEM, NO HALLUCINOGENS.
CAUSES OF DEATH, RUPTURED SKULL, CEREBRAL HAEMORRHAGING AND INTERNAL BLEEDING.
HUH.
THERE WAS A SMALL FOREIGN OBJECT UNDER HER NAIL.

MIGHT BE SOMETHING.
IT MIGHT NOT.
WHAT DO YOU THINK THIS IS?
COULD BE SKIN TISSUE FROM A SUSPECT...
IT COULD BE ANY FABRIC IN THE WORLD.
BUT EVEN THE SMALLEST CLUE WOULD HELP THIS CASE.

NOW, WHY WOULD SHE COMMIT SUICIDE IN THE LIBRARY?
TAP
YOU RECKON A BOOK JUST BORED HER TO DEATH?
HA-HA-HA
하하하
AH.
A BOOK INDEED.

COULD THIS PARTICLE BE PAPER? FROM A BOOK?!
MAYBE SHE SAW THE MURDERER, AND SCRATCHED THE BOOK IN FEAR?
BUT, THERE WERE NO OPEN BOOKS IN ANY OF THE CRIME SCENE PHOTOS.
THE MURDERER COULD'VE MOVED THE BOOK! BUT THE FINGER PRINTS SHOULD STILL BE THERE.

DO WE HAVE THE LAB RESULTS?
SOON.
JI-WAN!
쾅
BANG
JUMP UP
AIEEEE!
YOU PROMISED YOU WOULDN'T JOKE AROUND LIKE THAT ANYMORE! WE ALMOST PUT YOU IN THE FREEZER LAST TIME!

FREEZER?
I FELL ASLEEP NEXT TO THE DEAD BODY.
SO? WHAT'S THE VERDICT?
AH, YES.
IT'S ODD, BUT THE RESULTS ARE CONSISTENT WITH ANIMAL PROTEIN. THEREFORE, IT'S THE SKIN OF A DEAD ANIMAL.
D-DEAD ANIMAL?

OKAY, SO YOU MEAN TO TELL ME THAT IT HAS NO PLANT PROPERTIES?
Y-YES.
COUGH COUGH
HMMM.
AHHHHHH! IT JUST GETS WORSE! IS IT A SIMPLE SUICIDE?!!
WELL, GOOD LUCK WITH THAT!
Cheer up.

SO...
THERE'S NO DOUBT ANYMORE. I PROCESS THIS CASE AS A SUICIDE, RIGHT?
Bless me.
HUG
Umm, okay...
SQUEEZE
NO! WAIT!
WHIZ
DON'T MAKE A HASTY DECISION!
I HAVE AN IDEA. CAN I OPEN A SUICIDE CASE THAT WAS CLOSED 10 YEARS AGO?

DO YOU REALLY BELIEVE THIS CASE HAS ANY CONNECTION TO YOUR FRIEND'S ACCIDENT?
I THINK YOUR MIND'S PLAYING TRICKS ON YOU.

PLEASE.
HUMOR ME...

YO, KYUNG-DO LEE! I HEARD YOU SAW HER HEAD BLOWN UP! HUH?
IS THERE REALLY A GHOST IN THE LIBRARY?
WHY? YOU LOOKING FOR A HOT DATE?
EEK... THEY'RE ALL SO PATHETIC.
WILL YOU COME WITH ME SOMEWHERE?

I'VE FOUND PEOPLE WHO KNOW WHAT TO DO WITH IT.
ABOUT THE BOOK...
T-THAT'S GREAT!
THE BOOK...
...SCARES ME, TOO.

SO... WILL YOU?
YES, I'LL GO WITH YOU.
NOW...
...WE CAN FINALLY GET RID OF THE BOOK!

Originally the book was born
by a desire to live forever. Don't
forget all books in the world have
power like this. At the moment
when you read a page, it takes
your soul to specific place
and time. And then you will
see the truth of that place.

[Illustration: Hieronymus Bosch]

KYUNG-DO? ARE YOU HOME?

SQEEK
SQEEK
HEY, KYUNG-DO.

HONEY?

MOM?
AH, KYUNG-DO.
SORRY, SON.
IT'S BEEN A HARD DAY...
WOULD YOU LIKE DINNER, NOW?

THERE'S SOMEWHERE I NEED TO GO.
AND MOM, THIS IS MY FRIEND...
HUH? WHERE'S YOUR FRIEND?
HELLO! NICE TO MEET YOU, MRS. LEE!

THIS IS MY CLASSMATE, EUN-SAE.
I SEE...
...I SEE.

WOW, YOU HAVE TONS OF BOOKS AT HOME.
MY FATHER LOVED THEM.
SO, WHERE ARE WE GOING?
READING CLUB
IT'S KINDA CREEPY.

WELL, WELL.
HOW COULD YOU FND IT?
I FOUND YOUR CARD IN MY FATHER'S STUDY.
OH, WOW!
NO.
I MEANT THE BOOK.
IT HAS A WAY OF APPEARING IN THE STRANGEST PLACES...

I SHOULD BE ASKING YOU THAT QUESTION. YOU TOOK IT FROM ME 10 YEARS AGO.
YOU ARE HYUN-JUN'S SON.

I FOUND THIS
IN MY SCHOOL LIBRARY.
SEO-HA HIGH.
SEO-HA
HIGH SCHOOL...
HOW DID IT
GET THERE?
HMM...
PERHAPS IT WAS
A COWARD'S
DOING?
WELL, THE BOOK
CAME FROM THIS
PLACE. SO, TAKE
IT BACK.

I BELIEVE THE BOOK HAS CHOSEN ITS RIGHTFUL OWNER.
OH, NO. REALLY, YOU TAKE IT. I REALLY THINK AN ELDER PERSON IS MORE SUITED TO--
IS THIS YOUR GIRLFRIEND?
YOU HAVE EXQUISITE TASTE.

PLEASE, JUST TAKE IT.
YOU'RE JUST LIKE HUN-JUN.
WE ALL OWE HIM SO MUCH...

VERY WELL. I SHALL KEEP THIS FOR A WHILE...?
...ESPECIALLY ME...
AH, I'VE GOT A QUESTION.

WHY'S THIS PLACE CALLED THE READING CLUB?
MORE PRECISELY, IT'S A *PROHIBITED* READING CLUB.
THE CLIENTELE OF THE SHOP DEAL MAINLY WITH OLD AND MYSTERIOUS BOOKS.
WAS MY FATHER A MEMBER?

HE WAS
A HIGHLY MOTIVATED
MEMBER.
READING CLUB
PROFESSOR?
THE BOOK IS
HERE.

HAS IT BEEN 10 YEARS?
SO, WE HAVE ONE MORE CHANCE TO DISCOVER THE SECRET...
YES, OF COURSE I'LL WAIT.
HURRY. THIS BOOK IS SINISTER.
OH, AND ONE OTHER THING...
CLINK

GET AWAY FROM ME!! ANNOYING THINGS!
THAT BOOK IS CALLING THE DEAD.

HYUN-
JUN!

HYUN-JUN...
ARE WE STILL FRIENDS,
EVEN NOW?
OR ARE YOU AN
ANGEL OF DEATH,
AND HAVE COME TO
TAKE MY LIFE?

ARE YOU OKAY?
I KNOW THE BOOK MEANT SOMETHING TO YOU.
I'M FINE.
SOMEHOW, IT DOESN'T FEEL LIKE IT'S OVER.
I DON'T THINK THAT'S THE LAST I'VE SEEN OF THE BOOK.

I'VE HAD A BAD FEELING EVER SINCE I SAW IT IN THE LIBRARY.
THE BOOK IS BAD NEWS! BUT IF IT COMES BACK, JUST RETURN IT TO THE READING CLUB.
CLATTER
OKAY.
......
CLATTER

DRIP DRIP
DRIP DRIP

AAUUUGGGGHHHHH!!!

SHHHHK

SHHHHK

SCHOOOM

[Illustration: Hieronymus Bosch]

NEXT ISSUE...
WHAT HORRORS TRULY LURK BETWEEN THE PAGES?

독서클럽
READING CLUB
VOL. 2
CHO JU-HEE
SUH YUN-YOUNG
UDON
READING CLUB VOLUME 2, ON SALE FEBRUARY 2009!
READING CLUB Vol.2
ISBN: 978-1-897376-39-3
UDON
WWW.KOREANMANHWA.COM

EPILOGUE
FROM YUN-YOUNG SEO

THIS IS SEO, THE ARTIST!

Brother

This is the first separate volume. Besides, it's totally horror, and nothing else.

Before I started *Reading Club*, my biggest fear was drawing the book too 'funny'.

SHHHHK

The moment I drew this...

If I pictured the most horrible moment...

Hey! How's it look? Isn't it scary?

Brother

Meh.

Brother

Is this more humiliating than horrifying? OTL*

*The shape of person who cries on banded knees because of humiliation (Korean teenagers')

I really enjoyed doing this!

Thanks To!

Now, I want to say my parents have been waiting for this moment for a long time, but my brother, Woo-Jin, is really indifferent. I want to thanks Kyung-Jin, who was very kind and helped me out with the material! And I want to mention my friend Do-Yeh, even if you didn't help me at all!

Writer Joe, cheer up and let's keep it going!

Thank you, editor Ekari and Wink's editorial department for all your guidance.

Please wait for my Volume 2!! It will be released soon!

EPISODE 1. UNBELIEVABLE WOMAN

EPILOGUE FROM JU-HEE JOE

EPISODE 2. THE MOST HORRIBLE THING IS...

This is our work style.
You'll have a story this week, right?
My editor

OF COURSE! TRUST ME!

LIAR! ALL LIES! RIGHT?
You Liar! Lie! Mom! Lie!

THIS TIME I MEAN IT! SERIOUSLY!
LIE
LIE
LIE

Seriously?
CLICK
Sorry...
CLICK
CLICK
Mom, you're mean.

Jesus! Seo is finished and she's waiting for your story now!
Oh my!

When can I get the story?
I'm so ready.
My imagination
Eek!
She's waiting??!!

Hurry Hurry
Mom poo.
Eek!
Smelly Smelly.
Well, the most horrible thing is...
Seo, the artist!

EPISODE 3.
SORRY, MY BABY.

THE END

ONIMUSHA:
NIGHT OF GENESIS Vol.1
ISBN 978-0-9781386-1-5
STREET FIGHTER III:
RYU FINAL Vol.1
ISBN 978-1-897376-50-8
STREET FIGHTER:
SAKURA GANBARU! Vol.1
ISBN 978-1-897376-52-2
ONIMUSHA:
NIGHT OF GENESIS Vol.2
ISBN 978-0-9781386-1-5
STREET FIGHTER III:
RYU FINAL Vol.2
ISBN 978-1-897376-54-6
STREET FIGHTER:
SAKURA GANBARU! Vol.2
ISBN 978-1-897376-53-9
STREET FIGHTER II Vol.1
ISBN 978-0-9781386-1-5
STREET FIGHTER II Vol.2
ISBN 978-0-9781386-2-2
STREET FIGHTER II Vol.3
ISBN 978-0-9781386-3-9

READING CLUB 1

Story: CHO JU-HEE
Art: SUH YUN-YOUNG

English Translation: Young-Joo Woo
English Adaptation: Arthur Dela Cruz
Editorial Consultant: J.Torres
Coordinatiing Editor: Hye-Young Im
Lettering: Marshall Dillon

■

UDON STAFF:
Chief of Operations: Erik Ko
Project Manager: Jim Zubkavich
Marketing Manager: Matt Moylan

■

READING CLUB #1

English language version produced and published by UDON Entertainment Corp.
P.O. Box 32662, P.O. Village Gate, Richmond Hill, Ontario, L4X 0A2, Canada.

www.udonentertainment.com

First Printing: Dec 2008 ISBN-13: 978-1-897376-38-6 ISBN-10: 1-897376-38-3
Printed in Canada